Drawing

With Numbers

Created By: **STEVE HARPSTER**

WWW.HARPTOONS.COM

To Cooper, be brave and strong when facing dragons!

www.harptoons.com

Library of Congress Cataloging-in-Publication Data
Library of Congress Control Number: 2014907782
Harpster, Steve
Drawing Dragons With Numbers-
written and illustrated by Steve Harpster

SUMMARY: Learn how to draw dragons and mythical creatures
using the numbers two through twenty.

ART / General, JUVENILE FICTION / General

ISBN-10: 0996019707
ISBN-13: 978-0-9960197-0-5

SAN: 859-6921

printed in Loudonville, OH 44842 U.S.A

Want Steve Harpster to visit your school and draw with your students?
Email steve@harptoons.com for more information or visit www.harptoons.com.

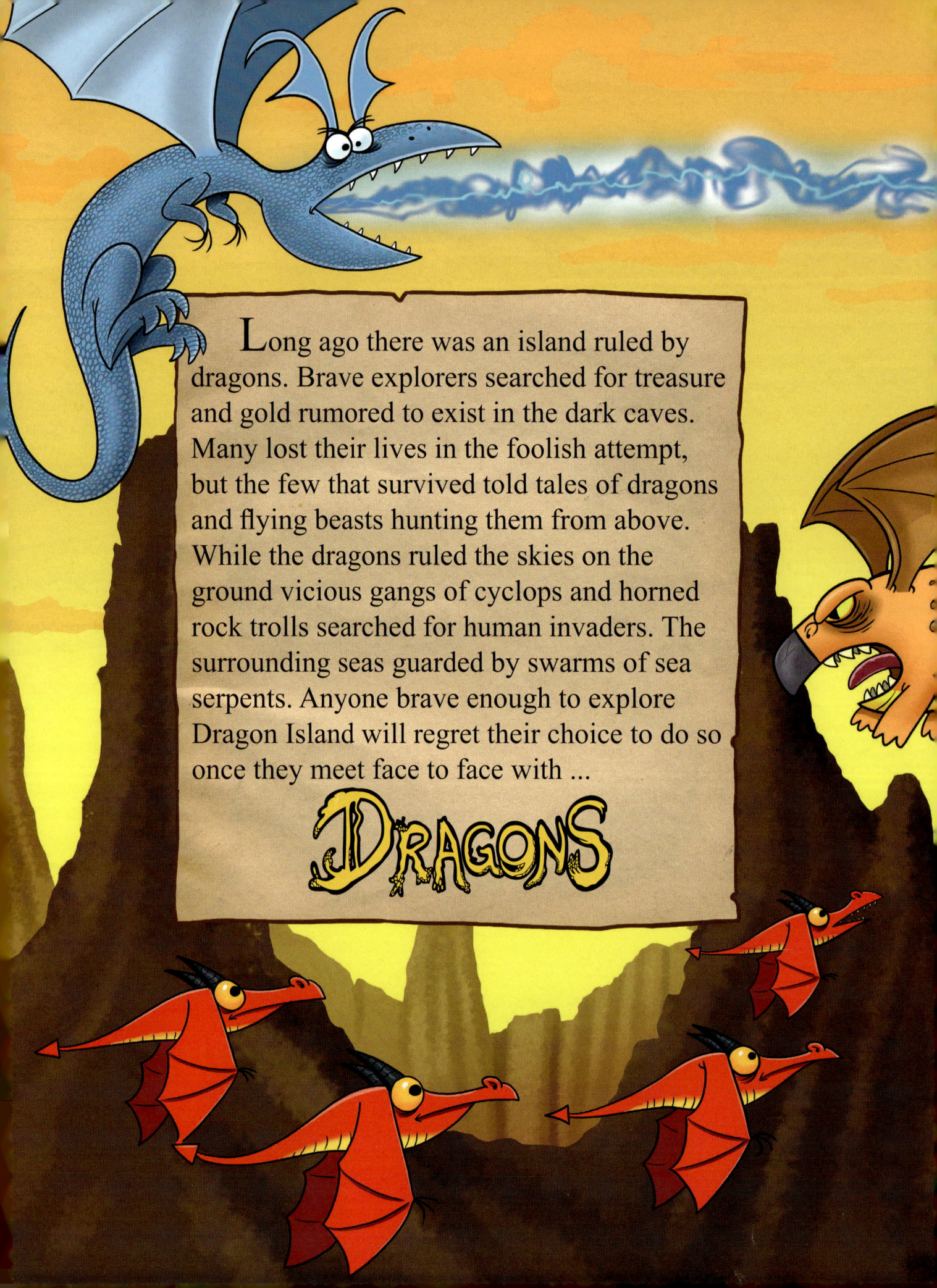

Long ago there was an island ruled by dragons. Brave explorers searched for treasure and gold rumored to exist in the dark caves. Many lost their lives in the foolish attempt, but the few that survived told tales of dragons and flying beasts hunting them from above. While the dragons ruled the skies on the ground vicious gangs of cyclops and horned rock trolls searched for human invaders. The surrounding seas guarded by swarms of sea serpents. Anyone brave enough to explore Dragon Island will regret their choice to do so once they meet face to face with ...

Dragons

Giant Smork

1.
2.
3.
4.
5.
6.
7.
8.
9.
10.

Horned Plated Dragon

Grunk Beast

1.

2.

3.

4.

5.

6.

7.

Flying Flurg

Sky Skimmer Serpent

Firey Fury Dragon

1.

2.

3.

4.

5.

6.

7.

8.

9.

Griffin

1.

2.

3.

4.

5.

6.

7.

8.

9.

Blue Steam Dragon

Cyclops

1.

2.

3.

4.

5.

6.

The Kraken- Patrols the seas around Dragon Island looking for boats to destroy.

Molter Mounta

Horned Rock Trolls- Live in caves and look for any humans to eat. They kill their food by crushing it with large boulders so it is easier to digest.

Sinkmerk Swamp

Grunk Beasts- Live in small herds of ten to twenty. They are extremely territorial and will protect their lands with deadly force.

Dragons aren't the only thing to fear on this island. Horrible sea monsters guard the waters, one eyed giants patrol the lands, and Medussa will turn a human to stone with her evil gaze. Any person attempting to explore this place is either brave or crazy!

Ship Wreck Cove

Medusa- Lives a life of isolation on Dragon Island. Her deadly stare turns people into stone statues which she collects in her garden.

Medusa's Lair

Garden of Statues

Cyclops- These giants roam the forests and have excellent vision, even though they only have one large eye.

Griffins- Can attack from the trees above or lurk about low on the ground.

Deadly Jungle

Slithering Sea Slinks- These serpents swarm the seas. Any ships with the misfortune to run into one of these creatures will be lucky to escape.

Swift Dragons

Medusa

Stone Mountain Dragon

1.

2.

3.

4.

5.

6.

7.

8.

Slithering Sea Slink

1.

2.

3.

4.

5.

6.

7.

8.

9.

Horned Rock Troll

1.

2.

3.

4.

5.

6.

7.

8.

9.

Green River Dragon

Purple Wasp Dragon

Cliff Dwelling Lork

1.

2.

3.

4.

5.

6.

7.

8.

9.

Flaming Red
Fire Fury

1.

2.

3.

4.

5.

6.

7.

8.

9.

10.

Kraken

1.

2.

3.

4.

5.

6.

7.

Green Boar Dragon

1.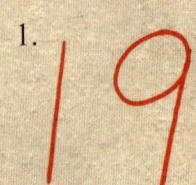

2.

3.

4.

5.

6.

7.

8.

9.

10.

Mythic Featherd Cloud Dragon

1.

2.

3.

4.

5.

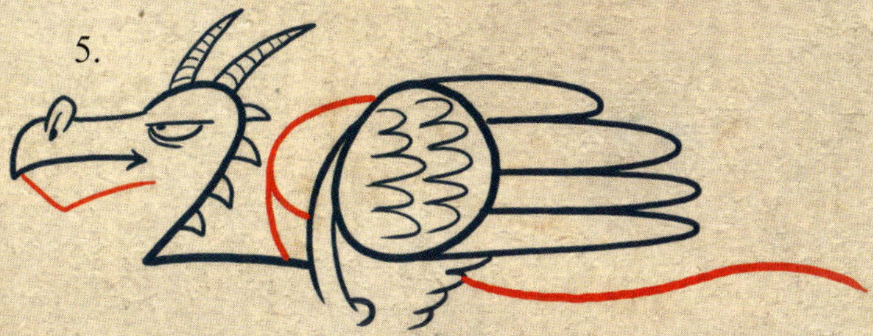

6.

7.

8.

9.